Isaac Asimov's

21st Century

Library of the Universe

The Solar System

Venus

BY ISAAC ASIMOV
WITH REVISIONS AND UPDATING BY RICHARD HANTULA

Gareth Stevens Publishing
A WORLD ALMANAC EDUCATION GROUP COMPANY

Please visit our web site at: **www.garethstevens.com**
For a free color catalog describing Gareth Stevens Publishing's list of high-quality
books and multimedia programs, call 1-800-542-2595 (USA) or 1-800-387-3178 (Canada).
Gareth Stevens Publishing's fax: (414) 332-3567.

Library of Congress Cataloging-in-Publication Data

Asimov, Isaac.
    Venus / by Isaac Asimov; with revisions and updating by Richard Hantula.
       p. cm. – (Isaac Asimov's 21st century library of the universe. The solar system)
    Rev. ed. of: Earth's twin? the planet Venus. 1996.
    Summary: Describes some of the various features of the planet Venus and how
we have learned what we know.
    Includes bibliographical references and index.
    ISBN 0-8368-3244-2 (lib. bdg.)
    1. Venus (Planet)–Juvenile literature. [1. Venus (Planet).] I. Hantula, Richard.
II. Asimov, Isaac. Earth's twin? the planet Venus. III. Title. IV. Isaac Asimov's 21st
century library of the universe. Solar system.
QB621.A82   2002
523.42–dc21   2002021800

This edition first published in 2002 by
Gareth Stevens Publishing
A World Almanac Education Group Company
330 West Olive Street, Suite 100
Milwaukee, WI 53212 USA

Series editor: Betsy Rasmussen
Cover design and layout adaptation: Melissa Valuch
Picture research: Matthew Groshek
Additional picture research: Diane Laska-Swanke
Production director: Susan Ashley

The editors at Gareth Stevens Publishing have selected science author Richard Hantula to bring
this classic series of young people's information books up to date. Richard Hantula has written
and edited books and articles on science and technology for more than two decades. He was
the senior U.S. editor for the *Macmillan Encyclopedia of Science*.

In addition to Hantula's contribution to this most recent edition, the editors would like to
acknowledge the participation of two noted science authors, Greg Walz-Chojnacki and
Francis Reddy, as contributors to earlier editions of this work.

Printed in the United States of America

1 2 3 4 5 6 7 8 9 06 05 04 03 02

Contents

Venus – Only One Planet 4
Phases of Venus.. 6
So Close, Yet So Far 8
Earth's Twin?.. 10
Radio Waves From Venus.......................... 12
Hot and Heavy 14
Earth and Venus: No Relation 16
Answers in the Echoes.............................. 18
Mapping Venus.. 20
Venus Revealed 22
Craters and Coronae................................. 24
The Greenhouse Effect.............................. 26
Fact File: Uncovering Venus's Shroud 28

More Books about Venus............................ 30
CD-ROMs... 30
Web Sites.. 30
Places to Visit 30
Glossary 31
Index.. 32

We live in an enormously large place – the Universe. It is only natural that we would want to understand this place, so scientists and engineers have developed instruments and spacecrafts that have told us far more about the Universe than we could possibly imagine.

We have seen planets up close, and spacecrafts have even landed on some. We have learned about quasars and pulsars, super-novas and colliding galaxies, and black holes and dark matter. We have gathered amazing data about how the Universe may have come into being and how it may end. Nothing could be more astonishing.

Of all the planets in our Solar System, Venus is the one nearest to Earth. It is very similar to Earth in some ways. The two are almost the same size, for example. For a long time, scientists could not say for sure whether or not Venus is a twin sister of our planet. It is shrouded in such a thick layer of clouds that you cannot see its surface. Space probes and technology, such as radar, finally made it possible to learn what lay below the clouds. Underneath its shroud, Venus turned out to be quite different from Earth.

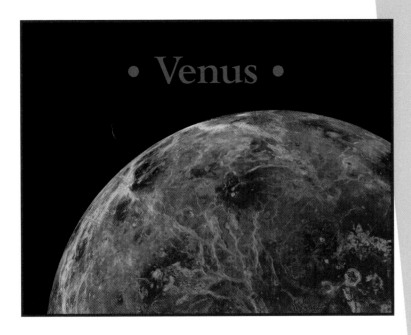

• Venus •

The Moon and Venus in a multiple exposure photograph over Tulsa, Oklahoma.

Venus – Only One Planet

Venus is the brightest of all the objects in the sky except for the Sun and the Moon. Unlike most planets, Venus never travels far from the Sun, and it can only be seen just before sunrise or just after sunset. When it is east of the Sun, Venus shines in the evening sky and is called the Evening Star. When Venus is west of the Sun, it shines before dawn and is called the Morning Star.

Ancient people thought the Morning Star and the Evening Star were two different objects, so they gave them two different names. Today, we know they are just one object.

Venus was named after the ancient Roman goddess of love because of its brightness.

Above: Venus, the ancient Roman goddess of love.

Phases of Venus

The ancient Babylonians noticed Venus's motion in the sky and became interested in the motions of the other planets, too. This encouraged the early growth of astronomy and mathematics as subjects.

Ptolemy, an ancient Greek astronomer, designed a method that predicted where Venus and the other planets would be in the sky at any given time. The only problem was that he pictured Earth, instead of the Sun, as the center of our Solar System.

In the early 1600s, the Italian astronomer Galileo Galilei studied Venus and found it had phases, like Earth's Moon. Sometimes it was full, sometimes half, sometimes just a crescent. The fact that Venus changed shape in this way eventually helped prove that all the planets, including Earth, revolve around the Sun.

Venus — a devil of a planet!

The ancient Romans called Venus *Lucifer*, which means "bringer of light." This was because when Venus, or the Morning Star, appeared, the Sun would soon follow. The king of Babylon was also called "the Morning Star." According to the Bible, when the king was defeated in battle, the prophet Isaiah said, "How art thou fallen from heaven, O Lucifer, son of the morning!" People thought Isaiah was talking about the Devil being cast out of heaven by God, so Lucifer became one of the names for the Devil.

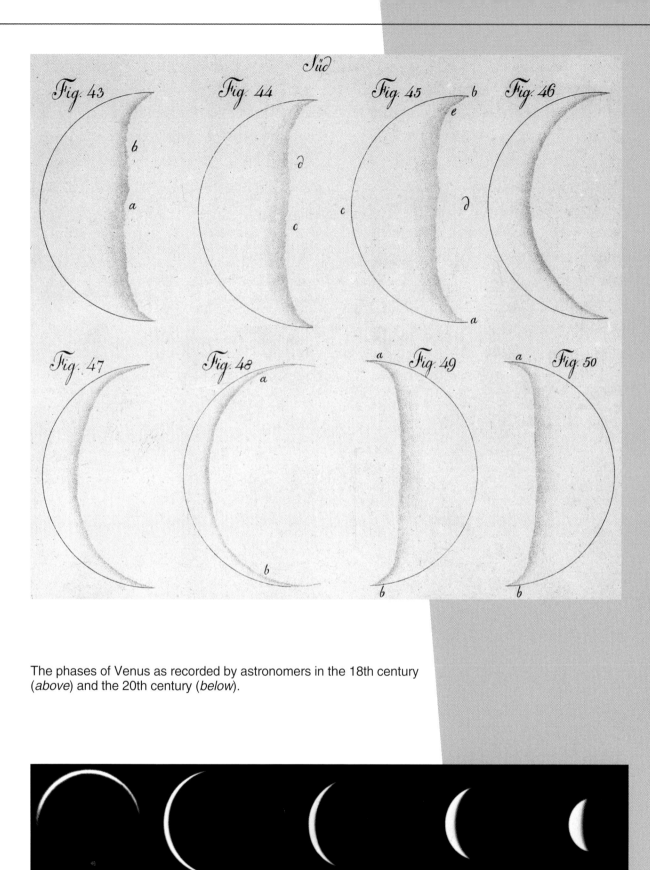

The phases of Venus as recorded by astronomers in the 18th century (*above*) and the 20th century (*below*).

So Close, Yet So Far

When Venus is on the same side of the Sun as Earth, it can be as close to Earth as 23.7 million miles (38.2 million kilometers). This is closer than any other large celestial object except for our own Moon.

In 1761, Venus moved across the face of the Sun in a rare event known as a solar transit. By watching this and other solar transits of Venus, astronomers could tell that Venus had an atmosphere. When Venus is observed through a telescope, the only thing that can be seen is a dense layer of clouds.

For many years, this thick cloud cover kept astronomers from learning very much about Venus, even though Venus is the planet closest to Earth.

Right and opposite, inset: In 1874, Venus made a solar transit — a rare event in which the planet moves across the face of the Sun. This solar transit gave astronomers a chance to examine Venus's thick, cloudy atmosphere.

Now you see it, now you don't!

From Earth, what can be seen of Venus changes as Venus moves in its orbit. Our Moon is at its brightest when it is full. When Venus is full, however, it is on the far side of the Sun, so it is harder for us to see.

When Venus is nearest Earth, it looks like a thin crescent and usually gets lost in the twilight. The best time to view Venus is between these two phases, when Venus looks like a thick crescent.

A Hubble Space Telescope
ultraviolet image of Venus's
cloud tops taken with the
Wide Field Planetary Camera-2
on January 24, 1995.

Above: From NASA, a three-dimensional perspective view of the eastern edge of Alpha Regio.

Above: Some people pictured Venus as a swampy world, much like prehistoric Earth.

Earth's Twin?

At one time, Venus's thick cloud layer made many scientists think that the planet must have water on its surface. Venus is closer to the Sun than Earth is. This means Venus gets more heat from the Sun than Earth, but scientists thought Venus's clouds might reflect sunlight and keep the surface of the planet from getting too hot.

Some scientists and many science fiction writers once thought of Venus as a young planet. They imagined it looked like Earth did in the prehistoric past and in the age of dinosaurs. They pictured Venus as a tropical world with warm oceans and an abundance of plant and animal life. Since Venus is about the same size as Earth, many people looked upon it as Earth's twin.

Earth (*left*) is close in size to Venus (*below*). Venus is only about 5 percent smaller in diameter than our planet.

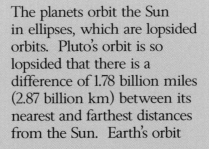

Venus wins the all-around prize!

The planets orbit the Sun in ellipses, which are lopsided orbits. Pluto's orbit is so lopsided that there is a difference of 1.78 billion miles (2.87 billion km) between its nearest and farthest distances from the Sun. Earth's orbit is much more circular, with a difference of only 3.11 million miles (5.01 million km). Of all the planets, however, it is Venus that has an orbit nearest to a perfect circle, with a difference of about 900,000 miles (1.46 million km).

Radio Waves from Venus

In the 1950s, astronomers began studying other kinds of radiation besides the waves of light. All objects, such as X rays, radio waves, and light (including ultraviolet light, infrared light, and visible light) give off electromagnetic radiation. Most of this radiation is not visible to the eye, but it can be detected with scientific instruments. What is more, objects with different temperatures give off different kinds of radiation. By measuring the type and amount of radiation an object emits, astronomers can determine its temperature.

In 1956, astronomers detected radio waves coming from Venus. This showed that there must be very hot temperatures on Venus or in its atmosphere — hotter than boiling water. Astronomers still could not say for sure, though, what the temperature on Venus's surface was.

Right: Radio telescopes helped scientists learn more about the temperatures on Venus.

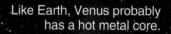

Like Earth, Venus probably has a hot metal core.

Inset: A heat-sensitive camera aboard the *Pioneer* probe provided this image of the clouds above the north pole of Venus. A dense, crescent-shaped cloud spirals outward 10 miles (16 km) above the main cloud deck. The bright spots are probably caused by rapidly moving clouds clearing away and exposing the warm atmospheric layers underneath.

13

Above: An artist imagines lightning flashing in an orange Venusian sky.

Right: In this drawing, a Soviet *Venera* probe is bathed in an eerie orange light on the surface of Venus.

Hot and Heavy

Scientists realized the only way to find out more about Venus was to travel there. In 1961, the former Soviet Union sent the first of 16 *Venera* probes to Venus. In 1967, *Venera 4* actually descended into Venus's atmosphere and sent back information to Earth. In 1970, *Venera 7* became the first probe to send back data from Venus's surface. *Mariner 2*, the first probe from the United States to study the planet, flew past Venus in 1962. Its instruments showed that the surface of Venus was at least 800° Farenheit (425° Centigrade). Later, scientists learned that Venus's surface is really even

hotter – more than 860° F (460° C), hot enough to melt lead!

Venus's intense heat and incredible atmospheric pressure put the *Venera* probes out of action, but not before they sent back a wealth of information. The information revealed that Venus's atmosphere is so thick that standing on the planet would feel like being at the bottom of an ocean. Scientists also learned that the atmosphere of Venus is made up almost entirely of carbon dioxide, with no oxygen. The lightning-filled clouds contain water mixed with sulfuric acid.

Below: The surface of Venus as it was photographed by *Venera 13*. The image includes the bottom portion of the probe.

Earth and Venus: No Relation

The probes all showed one thing — Venus is not a twin sister of Earth. The two planets are quite different in many ways. Venus is far too hot to have oceans of water or any form of Earth-like life. The surface of Venus is dry and desolate.

Venus's atmosphere is the opposite of Earth's. The air on Venus is 97 percent carbon dioxide with a little nitrogen and other gases. Earth's air is 78 percent nitrogen, 21 percent oxygen, and less than 0.1 percent carbon dioxide.

Heavy clouds reflect much of the sunlight falling on Venus, so its surface is always dim. Daylight on Venus is about the same as an overcast day on Earth. The clouds on Venus give sunlight an eerie orange color. The pressure of Venus's atmosphere is 92 times that of Earth's. Acid rain falls from the sky, but blistering heat evaporates the drops before they land.

Right: Venus (*foreground*) as seen when nearest Earth. The Sun and Mercury are in the background.

Venus, the planet of 584 days!

Venus moves around the Sun quicker than Earth does. Every 584 days, Venus gains a lap on Earth. Also, every 584 days, Venus is as close to Earth as it can get. Finally, Venus's rotation period is such that every 584 days it turns the same face to Earth. Some astronomers think Earth's gravity pulls at Venus and locks it into place. Earth's gravity seems too weak for that, however. Could there be some other explanation? Scientists do not know for certain.

Inset: Conditions on Earth (*pictured*) are quite different from those on Venus.

This illustration shows hot gases jetting through a vent in one of Venus's volcanoes.

Answers in the Echoes

The *Mariner 2* probe produced other surprises about Venus. By sending radio waves through the clouds to the surface of the planet and then recording the echoes, the probe discovered that Venus rotates very slowly. It takes Venus 243 days to make one turn on its axis, while Earth takes just 24 hours.

What is more, Venus rotates in the opposite direction of Earth. Earth and most of the other planets rotate counter-clockwise, from west to east, but Venus rotates clockwise, from east to west.

Left: Famous astronomer E. C. Pickering mistakenly estimated that Venus took only 21 hours to turn once on its axis.

Right: In 1951, R. M. Baum, an English astronomer observing Venus without the benefit of a radio telescope, calculated the rotation of Venus to be 195 days.

Right: At the rate of only one turn on its axis every 243 days, the planet Venus is not likely to receive a rotational speeding ticket.

1 rotation=243 days

In this illustration, *Mariner 2* determines Venus's correct length of rotation by bouncing radio waves off the planet's surface.

The *Pioneer Venus Orbiter* mapping Venus.

Mapping Venus

When radio waves are bounced off the surface of a planet, they reveal details of the planet's surface that are otherwise hidden.

Both the United States and the former Soviet Union have sent probes to Venus to map its surface through the use of radio waves. The most recent of such probes was *Magellan* from the United States. It spent four years in orbit around Venus, from 1990 to 1994, mapping 98 percent of the planet's surface in great detail.

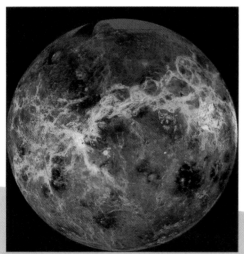

Left: This view of the surface of Venus was constructed with *Magellan* data that computers mapped onto a globe. The colors approximate those seen in images returned by *Venera 13* and *14*. The twisting bright features that cross the globe from the lower left toward the upper right are the mountains and canyons of the highland region known as Aphrodite Terra.

Above: Magellan begins its journey to Venus.

Venus Revealed

The terrain of Venus is divided into highlands and lowlands, just as it is on Mercury, Mars, Earth, and the Moon. Most of the highlands on Venus occur in just two regions — Ishtar Terra and Aphrodite Terra. These areas are similar to the continents of Earth. Ishtar Terra in the north is about the size of Australia and contains Maxwell Montes, the planet's highest mountain. Aphrodite Terra lies near the equator of Venus. It is about as big as South America and features a series of winding canyons and highly fractured mountains.

By an agreement of the International Astronomical Union (IAU), all features on Venus are now given women's names. The IAU is the organization that approves the names given to features on planets other than Earth.

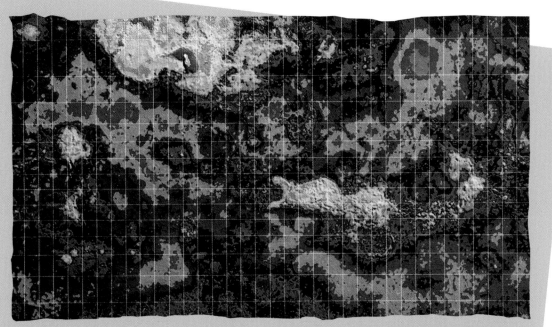

Above: A NASA map of Venus's topography, from *Pioneer Venus Orbiter* observations.

The volcano Sapas Mons rises in the center of this computer-generated view of *Magellan* data. Lava flows to the fractured plains in the foreground. The volcano is located near Venus's equator. Color was artificially added and is based on the colors observed by *Venera 13* and *14*.

Craters and Coronae

Mercury, Mars, and the Moon are covered with thousands of impact craters that have accumulated over the last few billion years. Venus, however, has only about a thousand of such craters that have been identified. Many scientists think an intense period of volcanic activity took place on Venus around 500 or 600 million years ago, filling the planet's oldest impact craters with lava.

Venus has thousands of volcanoes. More than 140 of them are bigger than 60 miles (100 km) in diameter. Among the many different kinds of volcanic structures seen on Venus are "coronae." These are circular features marked by a ring of ridges. Coronae can be hundreds of miles across. More than 400 have been found. They seem to form when hot material from within the planet rises into the planet's crust, weakening the upper layers and bulging the surface. As the area cools, the bulge settles back down, leaving circular cracks around the edge of the bulge with cracks running straight across it.

Somewhat similar to coronae, although generally smaller in size, are the spiderlike arachnoids. Other curious volcanic structures include "pancake" volcanoes made by very thick lava and insect-shaped "tick" volcanoes. In some areas, hot flowing lava has carved out winding channels hundreds of miles or more in length. The longest, called Baltis Valtis, has a length of over 3,700 miles (6,000 km).

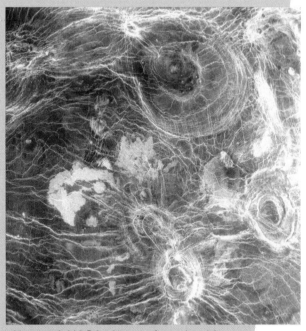

Above: A NASA picture of arachnoids.

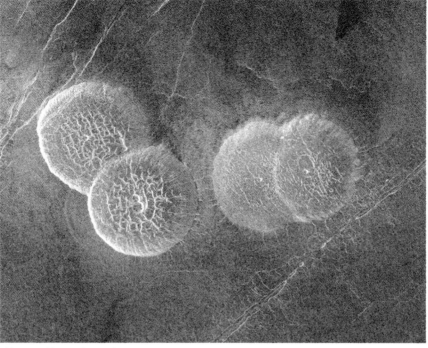

Above: Pancake volcanoes.

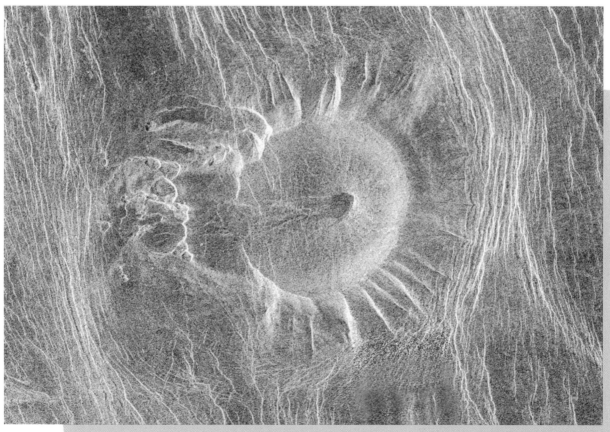

Above: A Venusian tick crater.

The greenhouse effect may have occurred in Venus's cloudy atmosphere.

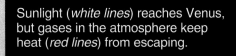

Sunlight (*white lines*) reaches Venus, but gases in the atmosphere keep heat (*red lines*) from escaping.

The Greenhouse Effect

Many scientists think Earth and Venus were more similar in the past than they are today. Venus now has no water on its surface and very little in its atmosphere, yet it may once have had oceans. If this is so, what changed it?

Above: In an actual greenhouse on Earth, glass walls admit the warming rays of sunlight but keep infrared radiation, or heat, from leaving.

Venus is nearer the Sun than Earth is, so Venus has always been warmer than Earth. Over time, more of its oceans could have evaporated, putting more water vapor into its atmosphere.

Water vapor holds in energy from the Sun. So Venus could have gotten still warmer, producing still more water vapor. Carbon dioxide in the oceans could have bubbled out as the water grew hotter. Carbon dioxide in the air also keeps heat from escaping. In other words, the carbon dioxide and certain other gases in the atmosphere acted like a greenhouse. This "greenhouse effect" could have caused temperatures to rise until the oceans began to boil away. In the end, there would have been no oceans left and a surface with temperatures as hot as a furnace.

The level of carbon dioxide in Earth's atmosphere has also been increasing. Many scientists believe that as a result, the temperature on Earth will slowly rise over the next few decades.

27

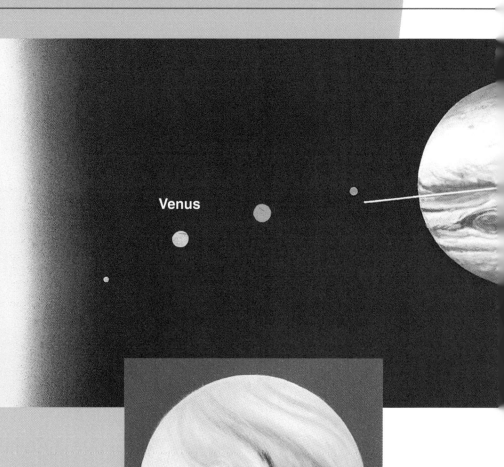

Venus

Right: A close-up of Venus. Scientists now know more than ever about the intensely hostile conditions lurking beneath and within the cloud cover of Venus.

Venus: How it measures up to Earth

Planet	Diameter	Rotation Period (length of day)	Period of Orbit around Sun (length of year)	Known Moons	Surface Gravity	Distance from Sun (nearest–farthest)	Least Time It Takes for Light to Reach Earth
Venus	7,521 miles (12,109 km)	243 days *	224.7 days	None	0.90**	66.8–67.7 million miles (107.5–108.9 million km)	2 minutes, 7 seconds
Earth	7,927 miles (12,683 km)	23 hours, 56 minutes	365.25 days (1 year)	1	1.00**	91.3–94.4 million miles (147–152 million km)	—

* Venus rotates, or spins on its axis, once every 243 days. The combination of Venus's direction of rotation and the time it takes to orbit the Sun makes a Venusian "day" — sunrise to sunrise — 117 Earth-days long.

** Multiply your weight by this number to find out how much you would weigh on this planet.

The Sun and its Solar System family (*left to right*): Mercury, Venus, Earth, Mars, Jupiter, Saturn, Uranus, Neptune, and Pluto.

Fact File: Uncovering Venus's Shroud

Venus is the sixth-largest known planet in our Solar System. The second-closest planet to the Sun, Venus never travels very far away from the Sun. That is why it can only be seen just before the Sun rises or just after the Sun sets. Venus is known as the Morning Star during its appearance before dawn and the Evening Star during its appearance after dusk.

Venus is the brightest of all the planets and stars. Only the Sun and Earth's Moon are brighter. In fact, there have been reports of Venus "shining" brightly enough on a moonless night to cast shadows on Earth.

More is known about Venus today than ever before. Beginning in the 1960s, probes studied the surface of Venus, its atmosphere, and its thick layer of clouds. It is this thick layer of clouds that obscures Venus's surface, gives the planet its bright appearance, and holds in the intense heat of the Sun. Venus is no longer thought of as Earth's mysterious twin, yet it remains one of the most beautiful and intriguing objects gracing the sky.

More Books about Venus

DK Space Encyclopedia. Nigel Henbest and Heather Couper (DK Publishing)

A Look at Venus. Ray Spangenburg and Kit Moser (Franklin Watts)

Venus. Seymour Simon (William Morrow)

Venus. Gregory Vogt (Millbrook)

Venus: The Second Planet. Michael D. Cole (Enslow)

CD-ROMs

Exploring the Planets. (Cinegram)

Web Sites

The Internet is a good place to get more information about Venus. The web sites listed here can help you learn about the most recent discoveries, as well as those made in the past.

Magellan Mission to Venus. www.jpl.nasa.gov/magellan/

Nine Planets. www.nineplanets.org/venus.html

Views of the Solar System. www.solarviews.com/eng/venus.htm

Windows to the Universe. www.windows.ucar.edu/tour/link=/venus/venus.html

Places to Visit

Here are some museums and centers where you can find a variety of space exhibits.

American Museum of Natural History
Central Park West at 79th Street
New York, NY 10024

Canada Science and Technology Museum
1867 St. Laurent Boulevard
Science Park
100 Queen's Park
Ottawa, Ontario K1G 5A3
Canada

National Air and Space Museum
Smithsonian Institution
7th and Independence Avenue SW
Washington, DC 20560

Odyssium
11211 142nd Street
Edmonton, Alberta T5M 4A1
Canada

Sydney Observatory
Observatory Hill
Sydney, New South Wales 2000
Australia

Scienceworks Museum
2 Booker Street
Spotswood
Melbourne, Victoria 3015
Australia

Glossary

Aphrodite Terra: one of the two "continents" on Venus. It is named for Aphrodite, the ancient Greek goddess of love.

atmosphere: the gases surrounding a planet, star, or moon. The atmosphere of Venus contains mostly carbon dioxide. Other gases present include nitrogen, plus tiny amounts of such gases as sulfur dioxide and argon.

axis: the imaginary straight line around which a planet, star, or moon turns or rotates.

carbon dioxide: a heavy, colorless gas. When humans and other animals breathe, they exhale carbon dioxide.

coronae: on Venus, a large oval or circular volcanic structure surrounded by a ring of ridges and marked by cracks running straight across it. Coronae can be hundreds of miles wide.

craters: holes on planets and moons created by volcanic activity or the impact of meteorites.

Evening Star: the name by which Venus has long been known when it appears in the evening sky.

gravity: the force that causes objects like the Sun and its planets to be attracted to one another.

greenhouse effect: the trapping of heat by a planet's atmosphere, causing the temperature at the planet's surface to gradually rise.

Ishtar Terra: one of the two "continents" on Venus. It is named for Ishtar, the ancient Babylonian goddess of love.

Lucifer: a Latin name meaning "bearer of light." It is applied both to Venus as the Morning Star (because it rises before the Sun) and to the Devil (as the most glorious of angels before being cast out of heaven).

Magellan: a space probe that was launched in 1989 and orbited Venus from 1990 to 1994, when it burned up in the planet's atmosphere. It mapped almost the entire surface of the planet.

Morning Star: the name by which Venus has long been known when it appears in the morning sky.

orbit: the path that one celestial object follows as it circles or revolves around another.

planet: one of the large bodies that revolve around a star like our Sun. Our Earth and Venus are planets in our Solar System.

radio telescope: an instrument that uses a radio receiver and antenna to see into space.

Solar System: the Sun with the planets and all the other bodies, such as asteroids, that orbit the Sun.

solar transit: the passing of a planet or smaller celestial body across the face of the Sun.

sulfuric acid: a corrosive liquid able to dissolve solid rock. It is found in Venus's atmosphere, making Venus one place where there is literally "acid rain."

Sun: our star and the provider of the energy that makes life possible on Earth.

Venus: the ancient Roman goddess of love. The planet Venus was named after her.

Index

Alpha Regio 10
Aphrodite Terra 21, 22
arachnoids 24
atmosphere of Venus 8–9,
    12–13, 14–15, 16, 26–27,
    29
axis, Venus's 18

Babylonians, ancient 6
Baum, R. M. 18

"continents" of Venus 22
coronae 24–25
craters 24–25

Evening Star, Venus as 5, 29

Galilei, Galileo 6
gravity 16, 28
Greeks, ancient 6
greenhouse effect 26–27

infrared radiation 12, 27
International astronomical
    Union (IAU) 22
Ishtar Terra 22

Lucifer 6

Magellan (probe) 20–21,
    22–23
Mariner 2 15, 18–19
Maxwell Montes 22
Moon, Earth's 4, 5, 6, 8, 29
Morning Star, Venus as 5,
    6, 29

orbit, Pluto's 11
orbit, Venus's 8, 11, 28

pancake volcanoes 24
phases of Venus 6–7
Pickering, E. C. 18
Pioneer Venus Orbiter 20
Ptolemy 6

radio telescopes 12, 18
radio waves 12, 18–19, 21
Romans, ancient 6

Sapas Mons 23
Solar System 6, 28–29
solar transits 8–9
Sun 5, 6, 8, 11, 16, 26–27,
    28–29

tick volcanoes 24–25

ultraviolet radiation 12

Venera probes 14–15, 21, 23
Venus (ancient Roman
    goddess of love) 5
volcanoes, Venus's 17, 23,
    24–25

X rays 12

Born in 1920, Isaac Asimov came to the United States as a young boy from his native Russia. As a young man, he was a student of biochemistry. In time, he became one of the most productive writers the world has ever known. His books cover a spectrum of topics, including science, history, language theory, fantasy, and science fiction. His brilliant imagination gained him the respect and admiration of adults and children alike. Sadly, Isaac Asimov died shortly after the publication of the first edition of *Isaac Asimov's Library of the Universe.*

The publishers wish to thank the following for permission to reproduce copyright material: front cover, 3, NASA/JPL; 4, © William P. Sterne, Jr.; 5, © Keith Ward 1990; 7 (lower), Courtesy of New Mexico State University Observatory; 8, 9 (inset), Yerkes Observatory; 9 (large), L. Esposito (University of Colorado, Boulder), and NASA; 10 (upper), NASA; 10 (lower), © MariLynn Flynn 1990; 11 (both), NASA; 12, Naval Research Laboratory; 13 (large), © Paul Dimare 1990; 13 (inset), NASA; 14 (upper), © MariLynn Flynn 1990; 14 (lower), © David Hardy; 15, © Sovfoto; 16, © Julian Baum 1990; 17 (large), © MariLynn Flynn 1987; 17 (inset), © Matthew Groshek 1980; 18 (upper), Yerkes Observatory; 18 (center), Courtesy of Richard Baum; 18 (lower), © Rick Karpinski/DeWalt and Associates; 19, © Garret Moore 1990; 20 (large), 25 (lower), National Space Science Data Center and The Magellan Experiment Principal Investigator, Dr. Gordon H. Pettengill, The Magellan Project; 20 (inset), NASA; 21 (upper), © Sky and Space 1991; 21 (lower), 22, 23, 24, NASA; 25 (upper), © Calvin J. Hamilton; 26 (large), NASA; 26 (inset), © Garret Moore 1989; 27, Courtesy of Mitchell Park Conservatory; 28, © Thomas O. Miller/Studio "X"; 28-29 (all), © Sally Bensusen.